Weather Wise

Clouds

Helen Cox Cannons

Heinemann
LIBRARY

Chicago, Illinois

© 2015 Heinemann Library
an imprint of Capstone Global Library, LLC
Chicago, Illinois

Edited by Siân Smith and John-Paul Wilkins
Designed by Philippa Jenkins and Peggie Carley
Picture research by Ruth Blair
Production by Victoria Fitzgerald
Originated by Capstone Global Library Ltd
Printed and bound in China by Leo Paper Group

18 17 16 15 14
10 9 8 7 6 5 4 3 2 1

Library of Congress Cataloging in Publication Data
Cataloging-in-publication information is on file with the Library
of Congress.
ISBN 978-1-4846-0544-8 (hardcover)
ISBN 978-1-4846-0554-7 (paperback)
ISBN 978-1-4846-0569-1 (eBook PDF)

Photo Credits
Dreamstime: Azathoth973, 13 (bottom right), Eaglexr, 21,
Jakerbreaker, 14, Mvildosola, 12, Nantheera, 16; iStockphoto:
Imageegaml, 11, JLBarranco, 18, scol22, 13 (bottom left);
Shutterstock: Alexey Repka, 15, C_Eng-Wong Photography, 13
(top left), elen_studio, 13 (top right), Gwoeii, 5, irin-k, 22, Jacek
Chabraszewski , 19, jeka84, 9, konzeptm, 8, Maria Meester, 10,
patpitchaya, 20, Samuel Borges Photography, cover, Zacarias
Pereira da Mata, 17

We would like to thank John Horel for his invaluable help in the
preparation of this book.

Contents

What Are Clouds?. 4

How Do Clouds Form? 6

Types of Clouds 8

Cloud Colors. 14

How Do Clouds Move?. 16

What Do You Wear in
   Cloudy Weather? 18

How Do Clouds Help Us? 20

Cloud Quiz 22

Picture Glossary 23

Index 24

Notes for Parents and Teachers 24

What Are Clouds?

water droplet

Clouds are made of many tiny drops of water. Each tiny drop is called a **droplet**.

These droplets are so tiny that they float on air.

How Do Clouds Form?

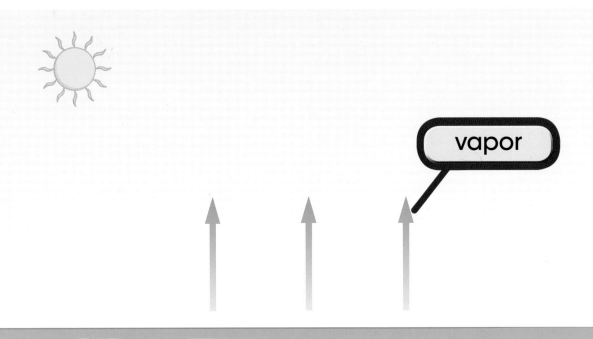

When the Sun warms water, some of the water becomes a gas called **vapor**.

The vapor rises into the air. Then it cools down and turns into droplets. These droplets make clouds.

Types of Clouds

Clouds can be many different shapes.

Some clouds are white and fluffy.
You may see these on a sunny day.

Some clouds are gray. You may
see these on a rainy day.

Some clouds are very dark and thick.
You may see these on a stormy day.

11

Some clouds cover the sky. You may see these on a snowy day.

cirrus

stratus

cumulus

cumulonimbus

Different clouds have different names.

Cloud Colors

Clouds look white because of light from the Sun.

Sometimes clouds can look dark and gray. This is because they are very thick.

How Do Clouds Move?

Clouds are moved by the wind.

Wind pushes some high clouds very fast. They can move faster than a car on a highway!

What Do You Wear in Cloudy Weather?

Cloudy weather means it might rain. You may need a waterproof coat or an umbrella.

18

Sometimes cloudy weather can still be warm. You may not need a coat at all.

How Do Clouds Help Us?

Sometimes water droplets join together in clouds. They fall as **raindrops**.

Living things need water to stay alive and grow.

Cloud Quiz

What clouds might look like this?

Answer: Cumulus clouds might look like this.

Picture Glossary

 **droplet** tiny drop of water

 **raindrop** group of droplets

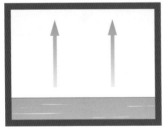 **vapor** gas created by heating water

23

Index

droplet 4, 5, 7, 20, 23

rain 18

raindrop 20, 23

Sun 6, 14

vapor 6, 7, 23

wind 16, 17

Notes for Parents and Teachers

Before Reading
Assess background knowledge. Ask: What is a cloud? How do clouds form? How do clouds help us?

After Reading
Recall and reflection: Ask children if their ideas about clouds at the beginning were correct. What else do they wonder about?

Sentence knowledge: Ask children to look at page 7. How many sentences are on this page? How can they tell?

Word recognition: Have children point at the word *water* on page 6. Can they also find it on page 21?